The ultimate bus...
from Bloom...

The new *Business Essentials* series...
pocket guides on a wide range of b...
performing well in interviews, to m...............presentations,
finding the right work/life balance, b........g up your business writing skills,
managing projects effectively, and becoming more assertive at work.

Available from all good retailers and bookshops,
as well as from Bloomsbury.com

Alysoun Owen is the author of the *Writers' & Artists' Guide to Getting Published* and contributed to *The Right Word: A Writer's Toolkit of Grammar, Vocabulary and Literary Terms*.

She runs a publishing consultancy and creates pitches, writes reports, and communicates with companies and individuals across various sectors and countries. She has been a commissioning editor for writing and language titles at Oxford University Press. Alysoun teaches a course on Project Management for the Publishing Training Centre, which covers communication skills and how to prepare information and documentation in a business context.

www.alysounowen.com

Writing Skills for Business

How to communicate clearly to get your message across

BLOOMSBURY BUSINESS
LONDON · OXFORD · NEW YORK · NEW DELHI · SYDNEY

BLOOMSBURY BUSINESS
Bloomsbury Publishing Plc
50 Bedford Square, London, WC1B 3DP, UK
29 Earlsfort Terrace, Dublin 2, Ireland

BLOOMSBURY, BLOOMSBURY BUSINESS and the Diana logo are
trademarks of Bloomsbury Publishing Plc

First published in Great Britain in 2022 by Bloomsbury Publishing Plc

A catalogue record for this book is available from the British Library

Library of Congress Cataloguing-in-Publication data has been applied for

ISBN: 978-1-3994-0213-2; eBook: 978-1-3994-0209-5

2 4 6 8 10 9 7 5 3 1

Text design by seagulls.net
Typeset by Deanta Global Publishing Services, Chennai, India
Printed and bound in Great Britain by CPI Group (UK) Ltd, Croydon CR0 4YY

To find out more about our authors and books visit www.bloomsbury.com
and sign up for our newsletters

Contents

Assess yourself: How good are your writing skills?

Assessment 1

Write down all the types of written texts you prepare in your job. Include all of them, from the formal to the more informal; those you write for internal eyes only and those that are 'published' to the outside world.

There will be more than you think. Concentrate on those that include continuous prose.

Types of written text might include (and this list is by no means comprehensive):

- company report;
- business or strategy plan;
- contract;
- blog;
- marketing or project plan;
- newsletter;
- public notice or poster;
- job application cover letter/email;

- briefing document;
- user or training guide.

Assessment 2

Now think about the ways in which you communicate in writing. How do you reach those with whom you are communicating? Tick all those that apply.

☐ letter

☐ email

☐ social media

☐ professional publication

☐ instant messaging

☐ online

☐ group chat

☐ PowerPoint presentation

Add any others.

Assessment 3

3.1. How do you feel when you sit down to draft an email to your boss or a peer?

a. Confident, I don't think too much about it, I simply get on and do it.
b. Sometimes I worry about the wording and find it tricky to find the right tone to use.
c. I always feel anxious when contacting my superiors and colleagues, as I worry about mistakes in my writing. It takes me longer than I think it should to draft an email.

3.2. What if you are asked to write something longer –
a strategy paper – for senior managers or for Board
members? How do you rate how you feel then?

a. mostly confident
b. sometimes worried
c. always anxious

Assessment 4

How good is your grasp of grammar and punctuation?

1. Do you know the difference in meaning between
    these words and in which context to use them?

    a. climactic and climatic
    b. affect and effect
    c. fewer and less

2. Do you know how to use a colon and a semi-
    colon, and how to distinguish one from the other?
    (Answers are given in Chapter 7.)

Assessment 5

Which areas are you weak in when it comes to writing?
Tick all those that apply.

☐ knowing how to start

☐ vocabulary and spelling

☐ grammar and punctuation

☐ structuring a document

☐ content flow and readability

☐ using the appropriate tone

☐ avoiding errors

☐ checking my work

☐ taking too long

☐ rushing – not spending enough time

Getting going

No one is asking you to become a literary sensation. The text you are writing is likely to be factual and practical. You shouldn't spend hours deliberating over every word and sentence. That would not make good business sense.

Having a clear sense of the PURPOSE of what you are drafting is the first crucial step in becoming a better business writer.

1
Why being good at writing matters

Communicating effectively on the page or screen is different from giving a presentation, contributing verbally to a team meeting, introducing yourself in person to a client or briefing a colleague face-to-face. In all these situations, it is highly likely that your spoken communication will be accompanied by some written materials. These might include items such as:

- a meeting agenda;

- minutes and actions produced after a meeting;

- an email to confirm what was agreed between two or more parties to record or clarify business discussions;

- a legal document to formally ratify business decisions;

- an email to thank, encourage or inform a client or colleague;

- a PowerPoint presentation to support a talk or lecture.

Getting your message across

In the world of work, getting your message across to the right people in the most effective way may be the difference between winning or missing out on a contract. It is a core aspect of doing business and should therefore be a priority for all organizations. The way you personally communicate, as a representative of your company or institution, is important. It will impact on how your company is perceived.

Good communication skills are beneficial because they can:

- enhance a reputation or brand;
- instil confidence;
- engage an audience;
- make you look professional and up to date.

Poor communication will impact you and your organization in negative ways. It might be 'poor' for various reasons. These include:

- sloppy text riddled with grammatical and spelling mistakes;
- badly formatted or structured documents;
- text that is unclear, too wordy, and not focused;
- content that is dull and does not engage its audience;
- documents that have not been planned or thought through in enough detail;
- documents that are sent to recipients without being checked for factual errors.

The chapters in this book, show how you can avoid being a poor communicator.

Companies that take written communication seriously may do some of the following:

- provide staff with training in writing skills;

- offer samples of good written documents;

- provide company-wide style guides and templates that staff should adhere to;

- adapt their styles, formats and means of communication depending on market changes;

- welcome feedback from staff on new ways of communicating, based on market response and data evidence.

TOP TIP

Clear and focused writing is not an end in itself. Communicating well, so that you get your intended message across to colleagues, clients or customers is an essential aspect of performing well in the business world.

You want your message to be as easy as possible for your readers to understand.

You don't need to be a wordsmith or literature graduate to write well. However, you do need to practise. Flexing your writing muscles can be hard but ultimately rewarding. You will get to a stage at which you worry less about including the 'right' word in your prose and have a fluency that allows you to adapt your style and approach to suit different contexts.

How you put your point of view across to engage, inform, persuade or sell to others matters. Writing clear, error-free content that is right for the purpose for which it is intended is something individuals and teams can learn to do.

This book is full of quick tips and nuggets of advice about how to communicate better in your business writing. It will guide you as you consider:

✔ the best way to communicate;

✔ the most effective format to use;

✔ the most appropriate tone to adopt;

✔ what style errors and other pitfalls to avoid.

Each chapter highlights an aspect that all business executives need to consider when communicating with colleagues or external contacts. You will be provided with the essential tools to improve the following aspects of your written communication:

✔ layout and structure;

✔ use of language: tone, style and terminology;

✔ spelling, grammar and punctuation.

The five Cs of writing

If you consider the five Cs as you prepare your texts, you can concentrate on getting your content right. That means making sure your 'message' is delivered:

✔ clearly

✔ concisely

✔ consistently

✔ coherently

✔ confidently

Over time, the checks you make on your prose as you write will become second nature. As you develop your skills and prepare new texts, use the Checklists at the end of the book to prompt and remind you of the key things to consider when you start to tap on your keyboard and compose a piece of writing.

Learn from examples

Examples of good (and not such good) practice are included throughout the text to illustrate where writing can be improved. Improving a text means making it more readable and therefore more effective as a business communication tool.

By the end of the book, you will be able to critically evaluate your own prose and so improve the quality and effectiveness of the document, emails or social media posts that you create.

> **TOP TIP**
>
> Interrogate the reports, emails and other documents you receive from others. What works, what doesn't?
>
> Are they clear? If not, why do you think that is?
>
> You could keep a file of best-practice examples of layouts, structures or phrases that you can use in your own writing.

2
Communicating with purpose

The key to all written communication is getting your message across. The text needs to be fit for purpose. It should be three things:

1. concise
2. clear
3. useful

Concise means to the point, free from waffle. It doesn't necessarily mean the document is short, but it will mean it says only what it needs to say.

Clear means the document makes sense and the intended reader can follow the points, argument or information in it.

Useful means that it is necessary to the person receiving it. An alternative word might be relevant.

Getting started

Before you start writing, you should ask yourself these key questions:

- Why am I communicating?
- What is the purpose of the email or document that I am drafting?

- Who am I communicating with?
- How am I corresponding or communicating?
- Is this the most effective or efficient way to communicate my message?

Of course, you don't need to actively do this for much of the communicating you do – e.g. pinging daily update messages to colleagues. However, do have these questions in the back of your mind even for the shortest of communications. Do you need to rush to reply to an email? Do you need to do it now? What purpose will it serve and is it the best use of your time? Is email the best way to communicate: would a phone call or a chat over a coffee next time you meet be a better way to convey your message?

Purpose

From the outset, consider your reader: this is the recipient(s) of your email, social media post or strategy report.

Consider these questions:

Question 1

What is the reason for writing your text? Is it:

- to supply information?
- to prompt action?
- to be persuasive?
- to sell a service?

Question 2

What do those who receive it need to do with it? Is the content of your communication something that the recipients have to:

- read and take note of – is it for information only?

- read and act upon – does it require follow-up, a reply or to be cascaded to their team?

- read and comment or amend – does it need collaborative input?

- read and sign off – does it have to be sanctioned by a more senior staff member?

Question 3

What is the status and importance of the communication? Is it:

- mandatory – a legal requirement that the recipient must digest before confirming that they have noted their responsibilities, e.g. an annual Safeguarding Guidance document?

or

- provided as background detail or discretionary advice?

How can you tell if writing is 'good'?

Good writing not only has a clear sense of purpose in the mind of the person producing it, but it should also be evident to those reading it what the text is for. A clear and focused approach suggests clarity of mind and a document that has been well thought through. Don't undermine valuable time spent defining a business strategy, only to rush to distribute it more widely in a document that doesn't pass the 'effective communication' test.

Planning what you want to say is an important first step in communicating well. In simple terms, having a beginning, middle and end for your text helps provide a structure or skeleton shape on which the details of your content will be fleshed out.

There is advice in Chapter 5 on layout (which is linked to structure): how important it is for readers to navigate your documents. Preparing what you want to say and how you might then structure a document is an essential part of the writing process.

The writing process: the 5-point plan

The steps in creating a report or other longer forms of text, involve:

1. knowing your market: thinking;
2. researching and planning;
3. preparing an outline structure;
4. drafting: creating and writing;
5. reviewing, refining and redrafting.

Step 1:
Thinking

Spend time thinking about the document you are going to create. Ask yourself some of the questions listed on pp. 16–18.

- Why is my document needed?
- Who is my audience?
- What do they need to know?

With answers to these questions, you should be in a better position to start planning your document. If you can't answer them with confidence, then consult colleagues for advice. It might be that the business has not defined these adequately and that some more discussion is required before you draft your document. For expediency, you could draft a document and place it on a share area, such as SharePoint or Google Docs, with questions attached to prompt colleagues into contributing their views.

> ### TOP TIP
>
> Carry a notebook around with you in which to jot down ideas. They may come to you when you're travelling or as you prepare other material; you don't want to lose them. You can use Notes on your laptop or phone, too. Mind maps and spider diagrams of linked topics to cover in a document can be helpful. Some might become headings in the final piece. Begin to think about structure – not in a formal way – but by sifting through the key elements you want to cover.
>
> Be disciplined with your time and coverage. Try to avoid getting diverted by irrelevant sub-topics.

Step 2:
Researching and planning

You may need to gather facts, statistics and other data from multiple sources to back up points you make in your document. Evidence might come from the market, colleagues or external literature. For example, the results of a recent industry survey or a recently published, peer-reviewed journal. Evidence that is relevant and of suitable prestige can improve a presentation and add business bite.

You may be reliant on content for some parts of your document from others, so try to have a clear plan on timings, working back from the date on which you want to circulate the document. Allow colleagues time to do their own research and planning for their sections and give them a clear sense of direction: what they need to supply to you, when, and how much copy you need. This will make things easier when it comes to collating their content with your own.

To get colleague input, it's a good idea to have your own plans in focus first. You may know broadly what you need to cover or even have a draft outline (see Step 3) that you can share with others. That way, all parties know what is expected of them and together you have a clearly defined set of criteria to stick to.

Example: I've been asked to prepare a draft business plan for a new service to be delivered in China.

After consulting colleagues in a kick-off meeting for the projects so you know what the reason for the document is and who will see it (internal stakeholders only or others outside the business too?), start to put down ideas on what needs to be covered. These include the standard elements around project aims and vision, set-up and delivery, impact and outputs, such as revenue and brand expansion in new markets, and a section on project review once it has been delivered.

Step 3:
Preparing an outline

Using the ideas from the research stage, it is a good idea to prepare a clear structure for your document: an outline, with headings. Include all the areas you want to communicate in an order that is logical. You can change the order of sections around later if you need to. A list of headings is much less intimidating than a blank page or screen, and it also helps keep your content relevant. You probably know much more about a subject than needs to be shared with others. Retain your notes so you can refer to them later, particularly if they provide useful background information or data evidence, but resist squeezing them all into your formal document. It will make your document less clear. Keep to the essentials. The outline keeps you focused on your document's purpose.

Depending on what your document is, you can order the sections/headings:

- in chronological order: highlighting the latest information first;

- in reverse chronological order: highlighting activities that have already happened;

- in alphabetical order: putting information of equal weight in A–Z order;

- in a hierarchy based on standard formats that readers would expect to see;

- in a logical, ascending order of importance that best suits the content you are relaying.

Having a strong outline will help you see if there are areas of weakness or gaps. You might need to do some more fact-finding or research to create text for each of the sections you have identified in your outline. It's better to know that early on, rather than when you are halfway through drafting a document, when you have reduced time to locate additional material, especially if you are reliant on others to provide it.

Example: An outline for a new training product. This includes a title, headings and sub-headings for each section in the plan. The heading styles may get modified later. At this stage, the different styles indicate the heading hierarchy, e.g. sub-headings are in italic and indented under the main headings which are in capitals.

PROJECT INITIATION DOCUMENT

Project: New Talent Lab

PROJECT DESCRIPTION

    Overall vision
    Longer-term project goals

PILOT

    Purpose
    Pilot goals

CONTENT & DELIVERY

    Format
    Full programme concept & delivery

MARKET & SALES MODELS

FINANCIALS

    Revenue projections
    Budget

BENEFITS

    Value to customers
    Value to company and brand

RISKS

PROJECT REVIEW

    Measures of success

Step 4:
Drafting your text

Once you have a structural outline, you can start filling in the detail.

You can do this in the way you find most constructive. You could fill in the sections you are most familiar or confident with first, for which you have material to hand. This makes you feel positive, that you're getting on with the task of writing, and allows you to quickly get some words down. That means you don't necessarily work through the document from start to finish in its structural order, though you can do that too: you'll find out the process that works best for you. It is likely to differ for the various documents you create.

TOP TIP

Before you draft a report or business plan, think about why you are creating it. What is the purpose of the document? As you go over in your mind the key points you need to get across, draft a skeleton structure. Define the introduction, middle and conclusion of the document. You can add further detail to this outline as you go along, but it helps keep you focused.

Step 5:
Checking and refining

Writing your document is referred to as 'drafting'. When you have a full first draft, you will need to look at it afresh and check the content and the style of the document. It is not ready to share until you have edited and reviewed it critically.

In Chapter 9, you will find tips on how to edit and check your writing.

COMMON MISTAKES

✗ You don't plan your text properly.

✗ You don't think about your target audience and tailor your writing to them.

✗ You get bogged down in waffle and try to fit absolutely everything into your document. Don't include it if it:

- duplicates information or a point you have already made;

- is not pertinent to your argument;

- is 'nice to have' and not essential.

If there is background information or evidence that you think your reader should be aware of, you can include this in an appendix or give a link to where these are stored.

BUSINESS ESSENTIALS

✔ Keep on target. Be strict with your text; don't waffle.

✔ Avoid adding in extra material if you can help it. Ask yourself:

- does it add to the points I'm already making?

- is it relevant to the document?

- does the reader need to know it?

✔ Make sure you plan things properly and consider the message you need to get across, your target audience and what they'll be using your document for.

3
Knowing your audience

Who are you communicating with?

It is likely that you will communicate with a range of stakeholders during your working day.

These stakeholders are individuals – or groups – who all have an interest in the project or task with which you are involved. If they don't, then consider why you need to communicate with them.

Consider who your main stakeholders are. Do they fall into different categories?

Are they:

- internal or external – inside or outside the business?
- known to you or new contacts?
- your peers, reports or bosses – more senior or junior to you?
- more (or less) experienced or knowledgeable than you?
- those who are essential to a project and need to respond and act or only need to be kept informed?
- located in your town, city or country or in another city or country?

What are the roles of some of the stakeholders you work and correspond with? Are they:

- colleagues
- customers
- clients
- third-party suppliers?

If you know WHO your message is aimed at then you can ensure the content of that message is tailored in a way that is effective.

What impact do you want to create?

Think about what you want to achieve by communicating with your audience. What outcome are you hoping to achieve? This will vary depending on who your recipient is. Think of them as your 'market' to whom you are selling your idea or point of view. Communicating well in business means creating impact.

It doesn't have to be dramatic, such as a global brand campaign via social media for a new product or service. It can be more modest.

Example: Providing clear information about a new internal training programme to colleagues.

Presenting this as a positive, supportive initiative and not something that implies criticism of staff's current working practices will be important in order to achieve the impact and outcome you want.

If your intended outcome, in this scenario, is to have 75 per cent of your workforce sign up for the (optional) training sessions within two weeks, then the approach you take in communicating and the tone you adopt both matter. Think strategically.

You can monitor the effectiveness of many forms of written communication by looking at data analytics:

at clickthrough sign-ups from a newsletter mailing or social media campaign and at Google and Amazon rankings. However, you can monitor the impact of other forms of communication, too, such as emails or written presentations, in subtler ways as you see how recipients respond or engage emotionally and practically with what you write.

Consider your 'readers'

Try to put yourself in the position of those with whom you are communicating. Look at what you are sending to them from their perspective.

- Is your message relevant to them?

- How do you avoid making them angry, even if the content might not be welcome?

- What concerns might they have about a topic and how you addressed those?

- Do you provide an opportunity for them to respond or communicate with you?

- What emotion or reaction do you want them to have on reading your text?

You will want to avoid making them angry or annoyed. They should not be left confused.

TOP TIP

Always think about the impact you are aiming to achieve with your document. What is its intended purpose for the audience?

Is it to:

- persuade

- inform or brief
- train
- market to
- sell to
- defend
- entrust
- encourage?

Have you chosen the best communication method?

Identify the method of communication that you think would be most effective in delivering the message to your audience.

Example: There is a rumour that your company is going to be restructured.

- Is a company-wide email a good way to deliver news of this?
- Might phone calls be preferable?
- Would cascading responsibility to team managers to communicate with their staff work better?
- What about a face-to-face or virtual presentation followed up by written details?
- Could a short set of FAQs, created in response to the Q&As staff asked at the in-person presentation, be drawn up?

Communicating with an individual or the crowd

You should also think about the number of people with whom you are communicating. Are you addressing:

- hundreds of people or a couple of individuals?

- people in several countries or just the UK?

- English native speakers or those for whom English is not a first language?

Are you hoping to have a dialogue with the person or groups you are communicating with? Will you need or expect feedback?

If you are communicating with a group of individuals whom you don't know personally, then the style and tone you adopt in your writing and the type of information and means you use for communicating are likely to be very different from those you'd use if you were corresponding with an individual known to you.

We will consider the appropriateness of the tone and style you adopt in Chapter 6. Does the size and substance of your audience and the content of what you are delivering have a bearing on the style you adopt? Should your document style be:

- formal or informal?

- serious or jocular?

- technical or introductory?

In all cases, it should be appropriate for the content, its purpose and the audience. It should always be professional. It doesn't need to be dry and stuffy. In fact, it shouldn't be; your audience is likely to switch off if it is. Being funny is hard to pull off and usually best avoided in business writing.

How much detail do you need to give?

Consider what level of detail is needed for the audience with whom you are communicating. It is helpful for you to know the following so you can tailor your correspondence or content accordingly:

- your audience's prior knowledge and experience;
- what the reason for your current communication is;
- if you want your audience to react or respond to your communication.

Writing about technical things for a non-technical audience

Distilling your expert knowledge down into a text that can be read, easily digested and understood by a lay or non-technical reader can be challenging. How much technical information and terminology should you cut out or leave in? How much prior knowledge should you assume on the part of your typical reader?

There are a few things you should find out.

1. Who your so-called 'typical' non-technical reader is so you know at what level to pitch your text.
2. Why the text is being prepared for them. Is it a briefing document to get them up to speed with the main areas in the topic? Will your primary audience need to share the document with others and so have a more detailed working grasp of the content?
3. How long your document can be or needs to be. You may have a restricted extent and thus any text you prepare will need to adhere to a required number of words or pages.

Think of yourself as a teacher who is preparing to introduce a new concept to a group of pupils. Try to empathize with them. What do you feel like when you are required to get to grips with content that is outside your specialist area of knowledge?

There are several other things you should consider when getting the approach right for a non-technical reader.

- Introductory lines to set the content you are presenting in context. You wouldn't need to do this for a reader who already shares your level of expertise or technical know-how, but you might for someone who is totally new to the topic.

- Defining key terms and specialist vocabulary in context.

- Presenting some of the content visually.

- Keeping your style approachable. Consider what it is you want them to have learned after reading your piece and make sure you achieve that.

- Keeping things concrete – avoid using abstract ideas and theories where you can. Have you got a real-world example that you can include to get a complicated concept across so it might be more meaningful to the reader?

TOP TIP

When writing about technical and specialist material for a non-technical or non-specialist readership, it is important not to bombard your audience with over-complicated material that is at too high a level. Equally, don't patronize your readers.

You need to avoid:

- over-simplifying complex text or technical detail – this could cause confusion in your reader and at worst, lead them to misinterpret what you have written;

● using too much jargon;

● including too many unexplained acronyms and abbreviations (see pp. 64–65).

Communicating with individuals with disabilities

It is important, often expedient, and increasingly a legal requirement to communicate well with all sectors and individuals. If you fail to acknowledge disabilities that some groups or individuals have and do not adapt your communication to their needs, you may:

● lose a customer;

● damage your brand;

● contravene the law.

Doing so suggests that you are not thinking enough about your audience.

There is little excuse not to be aware of good practice when it comes to writing materials for people with learning difficulties, dyslexia and sight impairment. Charities, government departments and organizations that advise on accessibility compliance all publish details on their websites.

There are now minimal standards that all companies are encouraged to adhere to. In the UK, legislation means that all public sector organizations must consider all potential readers.

For web content and printed materials, it is necessary to consider clear print to maximize legibility. This is not just about the size of type (or font) used, though that does matter too: 12 point is considered good practice. It also covers how type is presented in relation to white space, the colour used for type and what style is used.

It is best to avoid:

- jargon or long words that might be hard to understand;
- italics;
- underlining;
- fonts that simulate handwriting;
- unusual-shaped letters: in some fonts, an 'a' can be confused with a 'c' or an 'o', and a '3' can be confused with an '8';
- lighter type weights: bold or semi-bold weights are recommended for material specifically for people with visual impairment;
- decorative typefaces;
- words completely in capital letters;
- fonts where letters are not well spaced;
- aligned or justified text: align left for maximum legibility;
- complicated design;
- putting text over images and photographs.

It's a good idea to:

- use accessible language;
- use short sentences and short line lengths: avoid using hyphens to split words between two lines;
- keep pages clear of clutter;
- have wide margins and large fonts for headings;

- include lots of white space;
- keep paragraphs short;
- include ALT text on all online images and photographs;
- apply contrasting tones and colour when using fonts with tints: some people have difficulty distinguishing between red and green.

TOP TIP

There is detailed advice on how organizations can ensure their written communication is fit for purpose when it comes to communicating with those with certain disabilities.

You can find helpful information on these sites;

www.gov.uk/government/publications/inclusive -communication/accessible-communication-formats This includes recommendations on accessible communication formats, including print publications.

https://www.w3.org/WAI/fundamentals/accessibility -intro/ This provides details about web accessibility: how websites can be designed and the content on them prepared so those with disabilities can read them.

www.mencap.org.uk This is a good example of a charity that provides advice on its site for how to communicate effectively, including in writing, with readers with particular needs.

If you write in Word, you can run the 'Check Accessibility' function, which will suggest improvements to the content, format and layout of your text.

COMMON MISTAKES

✗ You don't think about your intended audience before you start writing. It's vital to consider who will be reading your document and to tailor your writing to their needs.

✗ You don't consider how your message will be delivered. Writing an enthusiastic post for social media is very different from constructing an email delivering disappointing news or writing up a report on a project.

✗ You fail to consider people with disabilities, or those with English as an additional language. You want your writing to be as accessible as possible, so it's important to think about how the font, language and presentation can be used to ensure everyone is able to appreciate your work.

BUSINESS ESSENTIALS

✔ Take the time to consider your target audience – are you writing for your boss, your peers or external stakeholders?

✔ Make sure you are aware of any particular points of 'house style' set by your company that you should adhere to – many organizations have company branding or specific values that you may need to consider.

✔ Ensure that your document is as accessible as possible and reconsider the use of jargon, idioms that not everyone may understand, or overly fussy fonts and layouts.

4
Some types of written communication

The range of business communication typically includes published reports and bids, through to internal reports, business plans, day-to-day emails and team briefings, social media posts and slideshow presentations.

How you communicate and what types of written communication you employ will affect your choice when considering the best format to use.

- Which means of communication will reach your contacts in the most effective way?

- How do you share, update or store your content?

- Is it delivered in print, online or via social media?

What follows is a series of written forms of communication with notes on what is good – and less effective – in each case. You may not agree with all of the points, but this should help you review materials you receive and those you create so that they are as readable and effective as they can be.

Example 1: Meeting agendas

Context: An agenda for a regular team meeting, attended by internal and external stakeholders based in several locations across the UK and US.

> To the Project Team,
>
> There is a meeting to discuss latest activities and actions for the Jolly Hockey Sticks Website.
>
> Meet my room, 4 o'clock on Wednesday.
>
> Cheers Sally, Project Lead

This agenda is poor because it:

✗ is brief, unfocused and very informal;

✗ has no clear agenda or link to previous documents;

✗ omits the date or time zone for the meeting.

Context: An alternative agenda for the same meeting.

> **Agenda for Working Group Meeting**
>
> Thursday 11th April 9am GMT
>
> Project plan here
>
> Location: [*details of virtual and in-person options provided*]
>
> Attendees: Sally B, Tom O, Jules K, Hakim N, James S, Nicola S
>
> Apologies: Mike T
>
> 1. Review of actions and status (minutes from previous meeting 25 March available here).

2. Course content, including sample (free) course.

3. Usage reporting.

4. Marketing communication.

5. Client set-up (new) and migration (existing).

6. Migration plan to new website – clarification of timings.

7. Testing.

8. Update on work this month.

9. Compliance (e.g. industry standard accessibility, GDPR etc.).

10. AOB.

11. Main concerns/issues and next steps/next meeting.

This agenda is good because it:

 makes clear where and when the meeting is taking place and in which time zone;

 provides context in the form of links to previous notes so those attending the meeting can remind themselves of what has been agreed to date;

 includes a clear, numbered list of what will be discussed at the meeting;

 suggests that actions will result from the meeting.

Example 2: Informative email

Context: A staff member emails a client.

Dear Graham,

Hope you are doing well and looking forward to the summer.

We wish to say again how grateful we are for the contribution you make to the *The Guide to Business Writing.* In the Editor's Note from the upcoming edition of the *Guide,* the Editor wrote 'at times of unexpected incarceration it seems people took solace in the written word'. It proves how our work as publishers and writers is as important as ever in ensuring that the solace, expression and escape which people look for in reading and in writing remains accessible to them. We hope that you are finding ways to adjust to the 'new normal' in our nearly post-lockdown world and to tackling the challenges which change inevitably brings.

The *Guide* publishes on 22 July, and we are working with our distributors to get a physical, gratis copy to you. Please can you send confirm that your postal address is unchanged – we have one with the postcode HP19 3TU saved for you.

If you would prefer, I can arrange for an ePub version to be sent to you instead once the files have been finalized.

All the best,

Tara

This email is not terrible, but is not well written:

✗ there is too much unnecessary text;

✗ it isn't immediately clear why Tara is getting in touch with Graham;

✗ the questions Tara needs answered would be better placed at the start;

✗ there are some grammatical and spelling errors.

It could be re-written like this. A more succinct message, relaying some key information and asking Graham to reply to two questions:

Dear Graham,

Thank you again for your contribution to *The Guide to Business Writing*, which publishes on 15 September. Our distributors will send your free copy to you. Please can you confirm that your postal address is unchanged – we have one with the postcode HP19 3TU on file.

Please let me know if you would prefer an ePub version as well, or instead of, the printed copy.

With best wishes,

Tara

Example 3: Formal letter of introduction

Context: A prospective author contacts a literary agent to see if they are interested in reading their manuscript.

From: jrush@timewaster.com

To: agent@literaryagency.com

Subject: Hiya

Dear sirs

I'm half-way through my YA thriller-western-fantasy noval and want to give you first refusal. I attach my favourite chapters, numbers 3, 9 and 15. I've not read anything like it before and all my friends say it is exciting worthy of being published. i trust you agree.

A spaceship has landed in Ohio on the night of the Black Hawk ceremony. Who are the strange visitors from outta space and what are they doing in the American Midwest? Do they come in peace or war?

I think the book will be about 150,000 words when finished and it will be one of a series of five books. I'm also planning on illustrating the stories myself and enclose some rough copies of some of me drawings.

I think this could be as BIG for you as other series such as Harry Potter or Paul Pullmans.

Cheers.

J. Rush

What's wrong with this email? The novel itself might be somewhat intriguing, but notice the following:

- it is not addressed to a named individual;

- it includes factual (e.g. Paul Pullmans) and spelling errors (e.g. noval);

- the tone is too casual;

- a random set of chapters and not the first three are being submitted;

- friends' recommendations are not a good indicator that a book should be published;

- J. Rush hasn't provided any information about himself or a phone number.

Here is another example.

From: linda.luck@gmail.com
To: agent@literaryagency.com
Subject: MS Submission: Carrie Brady and the Midnight Gang

Dear Susie,

I'm a huge fan of James Stride, whom you represent, and his *Light Fantastic* novels. I am sending you the first three chapters of my own YA novel, along with the synopsis and author CV as requested on your website for all new submissions.

'Carrie Brady and the Midnight Gang' is a 65,000-word novel that weaves magic realism through a contemporary narrative. Carrie Brady is a normal adolescent schoolgirl leading a life without adventure, until tragedy strikes, and her mother becomes seriously ill and dies within a few months of her cancer diagnosis. Carrie's mental health starts to unravel, and she drifts without purpose. That is until the midnight gang enter her world and whisk her away to places and experiences she could only once imagine. This is a story about triumph over adversity, a coming-of-age narrative of learning to cope with anxiety and trauma and the power of stories to heal a broken heart.

This book is inspired by my work as a counsellor with vulnerable young adults and their families. I was shortlisted for the 2018 Writers' & Artists' Short Story Prize and have recently completed a Pixie novel writing course.

Thank you for taking time to read the sample. I can be contacted by email or on 78000 00000.

With best regards,

Linda Luck
linda.luck@gmail.com

What's good about this email? Notice the following:

- it is polite and professional;
- the author has spent time researching a suitable agent for her novel;
- she is familiar with the agent's client list;
- there is a clear sense of whom the book is aimed at and where it sits in the market;
- details of relevant professional and writing experience are included;
- follow-up contact details are provided.

Example 4: Job advert

Context: Short job advert for freelance facilitators for training webinars.

This was the original version:

> We are looking for a highly motivated Webinar Facilitator for the Target Training Company to start work with us in January 2022.
>
> As the facilitator for the high-profile Target Training Company webinars, you will support our webinar presenters in order to ensure that the Target Training Company webinars are delivered to a consistently high standard to our range of clients across the globe.
>
> As one of our Webinar Facilitators, you will be joining a highly motivated team of people. The tasks you will carry out include: conducting pre-webinar technical tests on the webinar platform; introducing

the webinar and presenting housekeeping rules to both those attending and those presenting the webinars; running the webinar interactivities such as polls and exercises; chairing Q&A sessions; supporting both the presenter and attendees with any technical issues; ensuring the webinar runs to time and schedule.

You will be a calm personality with excellent communication skills and be used to sorting things out should a technical hitch or crisis arise. You will have your own computer with a webcam and good quality Broadband access. You should be able to work from home in a quiet environment. We would like you to be able to offer a minimum number of working hours for this facilitation role each week and month.

You will notice that it is wordy, a little repetitive and not very enticing. It is good enough, but the version below is punchier, shorter, and indicates what the benefits might be for the applicant as well as the company that is offering the role. The layout is better, too: using bullets to break up the text. It clarifies what the 'minimum working hours' expected are.

Webinar Facilitator for the Target Training Company (from January 2022)

Do you want to:

- work for a world-class training provider?

- support executives across the world with online training?

- enhance your communication and employability skills?

The Role

As a Facilitator, you will support our presenters to ensure the webinars are delivered to a consistently high standard.

You will:

✔ support both the presenter and attendees in dealing with any technical issues;

✔ introduce the webinar and present housekeeping rules to attendees;

✔ run the webinar interactivities, such as polls and exercises;

✔ chair Q&A sessions;

✔ ensure the webinar runs to time and schedule.

We are looking for individuals who:

- are calm problem-solvers with excellent communication skills;

- have good technical skills and access to a PC, reliable internet connection and a quiet location in which to work;

- can commit to a minimum of 6 hours' facilitation per week during the UK working day.

Example 5: Business-to-business email

Context: Email from the MD of a small production company to one of their freelance suppliers.

> Subject: Re: urgent query
>
> Hi Jim
>
> Rather urgently, please could you look at what I said yesterday (email below) and confirm as requested. I can get the content team to fill these gaps, but I don't want to have to play detective to work out what else might not have been done.
>
> This is urgent as we're about to move some units to the next stage, so please can you advise or confirm asap today/tomorrow.
>
> With thanks
>
> Susanne

What do you notice about the tone of this email? How do you think Jim felt when he received it?

If we add some context, does it make any difference to how you view it? Jim has spent several weeks working on the project and has not received any feedback to date. He has kept to scheduled dates, and he has always been professional and courteous in his own correspondence with Susanne.

Had Susanne adopted a less sarcastic tone and a more constructive approach, she may have received the information from Jim that she says she 'urgently' requires. Jim was unhappy to receive this email. It made him think his work was unappreciated. He did not respond well to Susanne's panicky voice: she was asking him to help her out but was not offering anything to him in return. His initial reaction on receiving the email was to ignore it and not be bullied (as he saw it) into a reply.

This is an example of an email that has not been crafted with care. Susanne has not considered the effect of her words. She has not maintained a professional tone.

This might have been a more positive email for Susanne to have sent:

Subject: Re: urgent query

Hi Jim

I hope work on the material is proceeding well. Sorry not to have been in contact before now to say how pleased we are with it. It is much appreciated that you are keeping to the schedule.

Might you be able to respond to the email I sent yesterday please? I've copied it below just in case it didn't reach you. I can get the content team to fill these gaps, if necessary, but it would be helpful to get your thoughts before I do so, by the end of today if possible.

Do give me a call if you would like to discuss this.

With thanks and best regards,

Susanne

What can these examples teach you?

How might you further improve some of the wording or approach taken?

COMMON MISTAKES

✗ You use the wrong tone for the wrong setting –
  your writing is over-familiar, you waffle, or perhaps
  you're even too formal.

✗ You don't make your point up front.

✗ You fail to proofread your writing and end up
  with factual, spelling or grammatical errors in
  your final product.

✗ You don't do your research before writing to
  someone with whom you're trying to make a
  good impression.

BUSINESS ESSENTIALS

✓ Always be professional;

✓ Err on the side of formal rather than too informal;

✓ Avoid trying to be funny – it may not translate
  well for your reader and may undermine the
  message you are trying to convey;

✓ Address a named individual – their first name will
  usually be fine, but make sure you spell it correctly
  (sometimes for more formal documents a full
  name and title might be necessary);

✓ Use a sign-off to suit the tone of the email
  you are sending (With all good wishes; Yours
  sincerely) and avoid very informal or abbreviated
  endings (Cheers; Ta);

✓ Never be rude. Don't use offensive or
  inappropriate language.

5
Layout and formatting

The way content is presented can have an impact on how it is received. Again, consider your reader.

- How can you make your text as straightforward and accessible as possible?

- What is the clearest way to present your content?

- Is text the best way to say what you need to communicate?

- Could you use bullet points and headings for clear navigation and highlighting, or graphs and other visual forms?

- Which fonts are readable, and which best avoided?

Consider the following as ways in which a document can be made less daunting.

Step 1:
Structure

Before you start writing any piece of text, consider the most logical order in which to put the elements. Your company might have standard templates or forms that will guide you, and there are many samples and templates online that you can adjust to suit your own requirements. If you don't have these, then spend some time planning your structure. In much the same way as you prepared an essay plan at school: it will save time in the long run. Keeping to the planned structure, assuming you have thought it through carefully, will stop you pulling in detail or anecdotes that are not needed for the arguments or business case you are making.

Sticking to convention

For some documents, there are some standard elements that convention dictates are included. Your reader would be surprised if they are not there.

Example: A press release for a new book.

✔ It includes the standard elements for this type of document:

- a catchy heading to attract journalists and reviewers;

- endorsement quotations;

- publication details;

- brief details of new content and benefits for readers;

- contact details for additional information.

✔ It is short – one page – and has visual elements (book cover and publisher logo and branding).

✔ It makes use of colour, bullets and bold type to highlight and display specific elements.

Step 2:
Dividing up the text

So that that your document does not put off the reader, avoid long, densely packed text. It's a good idea to segment key parts into separate paragraphs or sections, using headings to divide up the points you are making. These can be useful for navigation and design, too. You might present a main heading in a particular style, for example, in bold and centred, and secondary or sub-headings in italic, ranged left in a smaller type size. Being consistent with heading styles not only makes a document look more professional, but the reader will also know what level of importance each section of text has.

You can use some of these devices to break up your text in a long document of several pages or even in a much shorter email.

- plenty of blank space;

- short sentences and short paragraphs or statements;

- headings of various sizes and levels;

- bullet points;

- text highlights such as bold, italic or colour – though don't overuse these or a text can become confusing; use them to draw attention to key terms or concepts.

Employing such devices will also help the reader navigate your text.

Step 3:
Navigation

Your reader will be busy and may need to quickly skim your document, so make it as easy as possible for them to read and find the bits that are most relevant to them.

In addition to headings, you can use numbering to guide a reader through, particularly for longer texts with several sections. Stick to a system of either letters or Arabic or Roman numerals.

It can be useful to include a short contents list at the head of a document if it has several sections and sub-sections, hyperlinked to the headings in the body of the document.

Always number your pages. Documents might be printed out or an individual may wish to refer to a specific page: it helps to use the page number shown on the document rather than relying on the scroll-through numbering as this can differ on devices.

Headers and footers are useful for several reasons. They can:

- frame your document, giving it additional structure;
- make your documents look professional;
- include key contact details, document date, version and author information.

Step 4:
Using visual elements

Making a text more readable and accessible may simply mean adding an image or two to convey meaning or provide an example in a direct way.

Consider what might be the best and most efficient way to convey information.

Could you use some of the following to present data in more accessible ways:

- tables;
- graphs and charts;
- maps;
- boxes (such as the TOP TIP boxes throughout this book);
- timelines;
- diagrams with captions?

TOP TIP

Always think about your audience. As you structure, plan and write your texts, try to put yourself in the shoes of your reader. What might make your text more accessible to them? How might information be presented in more digestible chunks?

COMMON MISTAKES

✗ You don't consider the structure of your document. Think about which elements you want to stand out the most, and make sure the layout highlights these.

✗ You make things too complicated. It's tempting to use lots of different fonts, or a mix of bold and italic text, but this can often end up being distracting and confusing for the reader.

✗ You don't break up your text. Too many elements can make a document look cluttered, but on the other hand, you don't want to confront the reader with a wall of text. Consider using bullet points, text boxes or lists to keep the reader's interest.

BUSINESS ESSENTIALS

✔ Always make sure you include a title or heading, a contents list if applicable, and clear sections (think about numbering these).

✔ Make use of visual elements such as diagrams, images or maps if you're presenting data to the reader.

✔ Use different headings to signpost the most important points.

✔ Think about employing headers and footers in your document to ensure key information, such as contact details, is clearly presented.

6
Adopting the right tone and style

Words are the essential tools for all writers. The ways in which they are grouped and the particular words chosen are part of a writer's style. The style of writing used in a business report will be different from that used in a CV or a technical specification, a social media post or a promotional blog.

Tone is linked to style; it is the mood that the writer's choice of words and phrases evokes. There are three types: negative, neutral and positive.

In business writing, adopting a positive tone is usually best. A text written in a positive way is most likely to engage your reader and keep them hooked. You can do this by:

- using words with positive rather than negative connotations (positive words include happy, energy, empowered, appreciation; negative words include difficult, unknown, unreliable);

- showing appreciation (using words that invoke well-being in the reader: thank you, please);

- avoiding long explanations;

I will not be at the meeting tomorrow at 10.30 because I have another appointment that was already in my calendar, though if I return early, I will join part-way through.

Becomes: *Sorry, I'm unable to attend tomorrow's meeting.*

- including engaging anecdotes and examples;
- highlighting solutions not problems;
- replacing 'not' with other expressions:

  The office will not open. Becomes: The office is shut.

- avoiding 'don't' instructions:

  Don't book the client's accommodation until the date of the conference has been confirmed.

  Becomes: *When the date of the conference has been confirmed, please book the client's accommodation.*

A neutral tone may be useful in getting facts across, but if overused, writing can come across as dull, cold and unenthusiastic. It's best to avoid a tone that is negative and unenthusiastic.

If you are drafting a plan that you wish to persuade others to adopt, the content and evidence you include to support your case should include verbs that are persuasive (and positive) in intent.

The style and tone used in different types of text will depend on several things:

- convention – the style that is typically used and that readers have become accustomed to reading; this might reflect prevailing fashion or the limitations of extent;

- the subject matter – what material you need to cover;

- the readership/audience – how knowledgeable it is and when technical detail should be included or glossed;

- context – what other texts the reader might have access to;

- your intentions – how you want your reader to feel and engage with your text.

Voice

Voice is linked to tone and the overall effect your writing has on the reader. The active voice is when the person or subject of a sentence performs the action or verb: 'the boss held a meeting'. For business writing, use the active voice rather than the passive voice, as it will make your text:

- more immediate and direct;

- shorter;

- less formal;

- more engaging;

- easy to follow.

Below shows how the two forms differ. They can seem like subtle differences, but continuous text in the passive voice can render text long-winded and rather stuffy.

Passive voice: *The new strategy unit will be headed up by Miriam Jones.* (11 words)

Active voice: *Miriam Jones heads up the new strategy unit.* (8 words)

How do you know if you have adopted the right tone?

One way to find out is to reflect on the impact you have: the responses your get in reply to your message. Have you inadvertently provoked anxiety, caused offence, or given contradictory or incomplete information?

Are any of these factors important in the approach you take:

- gender
- age
- ethnicity
- social status
- economic situation?

You may want to adjust the words you use and your style (formal or less formal) to reflect the type of written communication you are sending. When you market or sell to consumers, you should know who your audience is. Your social media plan, marketing and brand activity will be styled to appeal to a specific demographic and their needs. That said, in all communication, however targeted, always be considerate and avoid any words and commentary that is sexist, racist, ageist, insensitive or offensive in any way.

Aside from undermining any message you are trying to get across, it displays an ignorance and lack of awareness. If you are worried about certain terms that may have connotations or potential impact that you are unaware of, ask others to check over your text. Publishers sometimes employ sensitivity readers to look at the style, tone and vocabulary used. Such readers can be valuable for other businesses, too.

If you are communicating with people across different countries, bear in mind that not all your audience will have English as a first language. Keep sentences short and use words that are unambiguous and that a non-native speaker is likely to know.

You should be sensitive to cultural differences and avoid subjects or terms that might cause offence in certain regions.

> **TOP TIP**
>
> It is a good idea to revisit your opening lines once you have completed your text. Does it pack enough of a punch? Does it suitably convey the essence of what follows, and will it grab your readers' attention? Could it be improved?

Keeping your readers' attention

Your intention with any text should be to keep your reader gripped and reading to the end. You can do this by including:

- a strong opening;
- stories that will capture their imagination;
- relevant and real-world anecdotes;
- a hook;
- a clear sense of progression;
- analogies to explain complicated concepts – make them plausible and don't overuse them.

Beginnings

The opening sentence or paragraph of a document, even an email, should be short and to the point. It is the writer's chance to grab their readers' attention. If the beginning is effective, the reader will read on.

Be confident

Cut out hesitancy in your writing. Persuade your reader you are knowledgeable and confident in what you are saying, through the tone, style and expressions you use.

Try to avoid the equivalent of 'ifs' and 'buts' in your texts and expressions that include 'perhaps' and 'possibly'.

Don't hide the sense of your text with woolly words. Avoid meaningless filler phrases that slow the pace and detract from the clarity of the argument you are putting across.

For example, avoid phrases such as:

I think that . . .
In my opinion . . .
It could be thought/said that ...

> **TOP TIP**
>
> If in doubt . . .
>
> ✔ look at how others have communicated well in business documents or correspondence and emulate them – model your documents on the best examples that you come across;
>
> ✔ follow convention;
>
> ✔ adopt a professional and slightly formal tone.

Vocabulary: the words you use

Clichés and redundant words

Clichés are expressions that become stale through overuse. They can become meaningless phrases that make writing less specific, less immediate or less concise. They are often figurative and reflective of an age in which they were coined and so might be dated, too. That can make your text appear old-fashioned. Figurative expressions, such as similes and metaphors, are also best avoided in practical, informative business prose. They may show you have a lyrical, creative side, but that is not usually a skill business correspondence demands to be on show. You are more likely to confuse your reader by making prose illustrative rather than direct and to the point. Similes, metaphors and other idioms don't travel well; avoid them in text that has an international reach.

Examples:

the calm before the storm
armed to the teeth
think outside the box
push the envelope

How might you convey meaning in a clearer, more specific way, avoiding cliché?

Example:

low-hanging fruit means something that can be achieved without difficulty: the fruit that can be picked most easily.

'Let's go after the low-hanging fruit in our bid to improve revenue.'

Would be clearer as:

'Let's target our existing customer base first to bring in additional revenue.'

The table below suggests alternative, shorter expressions that you could use instead of a cliché.

Cliché	Alternative expression
flavour of the month	Preferred or fashionable
food for thought	thought-provoking
steep learning curve	challenging
in the same boat	likewise or similarly
win-win situation	positive or beneficial

Each age adopts terms that become the buzz words of the day. They become overused. Try to find an alternative. Recent examples are:

fake news, big society, global village, boots on the ground, level playing field, new normal.

Redundant expressions

It can be tempting to use longer phrases in a bid to sound more professional, but this often has the opposite effect.

Avoid unnecessary duplication (the text in italic below is repetitive and thus not needed):

ATM *machine* = automatic teller machine *machine*
GPS *system* = global positioning system *system*
PIN *number* = personal identification number *number*

Cut unnecessary words – such as those in italics below:

original prototype – a prototype is original
past history – history is always in the past

Other examples: assemble *together*; *future* prospects; recur *repeatedly*

Cull filler phrases and words:

on a daily basis = daily
in order to = to
in today's world = now

Avoid long-winded, imprecise phrases:

it should be noted
as a matter of fact
as previously stated
it is significant that
one must recognize that
it has been determined that

Shortening words

These keep text crisp and simple and documents short where possible.

The main types of shortening are:

- abbreviations, such as *e.g.* for *for example*. Decide which suit the tone of your text and use them consistently;

- acronyms, e.g. UK for United Kingdom, a noun created from the initial letters of a series of words, and which has become a word in its own right. Other examples are NASA, UNESCO;

- shortenings, where a few letters are used instead of the whole of a word, e.g. *Ltd* for *Limited*, *etc.* for *et cetera*;

- initialisms, e.g. *Plc* for *Public Limited Company*, *AI*, *GDPR*;

- contractions, e.g. *don't* for *do not*. You should be particularly careful when using these; *it's* and *its* mean very different things, as do *your/you're* and *whose/who's*.

BUSINESS ESSENTIALS

Contractions have been used throughout this book. That was a style decision. A more formal text might demand these to be spelled out in full. Whichever you opt for, check your house style (see Chapter 9) and use them consistently and correctly.

It is usual to write out a specialist term or the name of an organization in full on its first use (with the abbreviated form in brackets) and thereafter to use the abbreviation. Use your common sense. Where an abbreviation is so well known that you don't need to spell it out, e.g. BBC, decide what is right for the reader. If you draft a report on GDP across OECD countries for politicians or a press release on the topic for political journalists, you won't need to write these out. A journalist preparing copy for readers who are less familiar with the terms may choose to write them out in full on their first appearance in an article.

Too many abbreviations can make a text unreadable. Consider your audience and the terms they are likely to know. Sometimes an abbreviation might need to be glossed if it has more than one meaning, for example: *CRM* can mean *Customer Relationship Management* or *Customer Relationship Marketing*.

Business abbreviations and acronyms

These are widely known and usually acceptable to use.

People

CEO = Chief Executive Officer
CFO = Chief Executive Officer
CMO = Chief Marketing Officer
COO = Chief Operating Officer
CTO = Chief Technical Officer

CBO = Chief Bottle Opener – that one is made up . . . but you can see that in some cases you do need to put text in full

Relationships

B2B = Business to Business
B2C = Business to Consumer/Customer

Finance

ROI = Return on Investment
MOM = Month Over Month
YTD = Year to Date
AGI = Adjusted Gross Income
EPS = Earnings Per Share
ROA = Return on Assets

General

BAU = Business as Usual
COB = Close of Day
FYI = For Your Information
IAM = I'm in a Meeting

Which others do you commonly use?

COMMON MISTAKES

✗ You use the wrong tone. Business writing doesn't necessarily need to be dry or formal, but you should consider the tone of your writing and how it will come across to the reader.

✗ You litter your writing with redundant words and phrases. It might be tempting to use several words instead of one, but rather than making you sound more professional, this can often be confusing or irritating for the reader. Stick to clear and concise phrases and avoid clichés.

✗ You use too many abbreviations and acronyms, or you don't spell them out for the reader. If you're confident people in your company or industry will know what an abbreviation means, it's fine not to spell it out in full, but otherwise it's useful to spell things out the first time you use them.

BUSINESS ESSENTIALS

✔ Always consider your readers. What is their background; what level of knowledge do they have about your subject; is English their first language? Adjust the tone and style of your writing to suit.

✔ Re-read your writing and see if you can cut out any redundant phrases, woolly language or clichés.

✔ Make sure any acronyms are clear and unambiguous – if an acronym can mean two different things, ensure that your audience will know which one you mean.

7
Grammar, punctuation and spelling

A basic grasp of how English sentences work is useful for the business writer. This means having a working knowledge of punctuation, the parts of speech and how to employ them in a phrase or sentence. Equipped with this knowledge, your writing skills should improve. Having an interest in words and how you can craft them into better, clearer sentences should enhance your business communication. The grammar, punctuation and spelling outlined in this chapter applies to UK English; US English and English used in other countries will have different rules.

Grammar

Text should be meaningful and achieve what it sets out to do for the reader.

Parts of speech

In English, we divide words up into distinct types. Some words have several roles or functions, depending on the way they are used in a sentence.

The librarian sorted the novels on the bookshelves into genres. (novels = books; plural noun)

The idea was novel; it was not one he had considered before. (novel = new; adjective)

The main parts of speech are:

nouns
pronouns
verbs
prepositions
conjunctions
adjectives *
adverbs *
interjections *

In business writing, you should be cautious, other than in marketing or selling copy, when using the last three (*).

Nouns are words for things or people; 'naming' words. They can be:

- single words e.g. *car*;

- compound words, where two words are put together to create a new word, e.g. *cameraman*

- or a noun phrase, where a group of words act as a noun, e.g. *assistant cameraman*.

There are different types of nouns:

- **common nouns** for everyday objects or a profession: *report, tarmac, lawyer*;

- **proper nouns** for specific people, places or geographical formations; these start with a capital letter: *John Smith, River Avon, Bank of England*;

- **non-count nouns** for feelings – you can't put a number in front of them to make them plural: *pleasure, grief*;

- **collective nouns** for a group of people or things: *audience, media, team, committee*.

Making nouns plural

To indicate more than one of something, you usually add an 's' to the end of the noun. Sometimes, 'es' is added, as in *boss – bosses*.

However, there are exceptions. For example, some nouns ending in -f, use -eves in their plural form (e.g. *shelf – shelves*).

Other irregular forms include:

datum (singular) – *data* (plural)
die (singular) – *dice* (plural)
criterion (singular) – *criteria* (plural)

The plural forms of these words are so well known and are mostly now used as the singular noun, too.

Data and dice are usually treated like collective nouns; they take a singular verb when referring to a unit (e.g. the data set is clear) and a plural verb when referring to a set or more than one individual item (e.g. the data were collected).

TOP TIP

Plural nouns

How do you know which form a noun takes in its plural form? If in doubt, look it up. There is no excuse for not checking.

How do you know which verb – singular of plural form – a plural noun takes? Some words 'break' the standard rules:

audience (which might seem like a singular noun, a single group) takes a plural verb; it is a collection of individuals.

fish and chips (technically two separate nouns; '*fish*', '*chips*') takes a singular verb as it is deemed to be a single noun unit.

Pronouns replace a noun or a noun phrase in a sentence. You can keep sentences shorter and avoid unnecessary repetition by using pronouns. Can your reader follow the sense of the sentence? If not, you may need to introduce nouns for clarity.

Example:

James Mullen will be addressing staff at the monthly briefing on Friday. **James** is happy to take questions from **staff** on all aspects of the new software implementation.

James Mullen will be addressing staff at the monthly briefing on Friday. **He** is happy to take questions from **you** on all aspects of the new software implementation.

> **TOP TIP**
>
> Relative pronouns
>
> ● *Which* refers to things.
>
> ● *Who*, *whom* or *whose* refer to people.
>
> ● *That* refers to people or things.

Verbs indicate action; every sentence should include one. In business writing, use strong, single-word verbs. They convey precise meaning without the need for modifying words.

Strong verbs make your writing:

● concise;

● specific (not vague);

● interesting.

Example:

Before you **carry out** the task assigned to you, you **should have clicked** on each of the links supplied in the checklist document.

Becomes:

Before you **complete** the tasks assigned to you, **click** each link in the checklist.

Tense indicates the 'when' of your action. You should use the present, simple past or future tense and avoid verb phases.

You are most likely to use the **present tense**. It can make your writing:

- clear;
- easy to follow;
- immediate;
- forceful;
- direct.

The **simple past tense** describes actions that have happened and been completed; e.g. *The HR Director selected the new recruits.*

The **simple future tense** states what will happen. A business plan might use this to optimistically indicate what a business hopes will transpire, though it could also use the present tense. You should avoid conditional forms using would, could, might, may. They can make text wordy and lacking in confidence.

Example:

The report **includes** information that you **might find** helpful and **could aid** your understanding of the topic.

Becomes:

The report **includes** information **to aid** your understanding of the topic.

The form of the verb you use will depend on the noun or pronoun that relates to it: whether it is a singular or plural form. Avoid mixing tenses or persons – it can cause confusion.

Prepositions show the relationship of one word to another, e.g. *above, below, under, during.*

Conjunctions join parts of a sentence together: *but, and, or, because.* Sentences that use conjunctions to link two points or ideas are known as compound sentences:

Our profits have declined in 2021 because of market conditions and our reduced workforce.

Adjectives describe a noun or pronoun, e.g. We have access to exciting new markets.

Adverbs modify a verb. e.g. Prices have risen steeply.

Interjections are single words that express emotion, e.g. Pow, Wow. As suggested above, use these sparingly in your writing and only when there is a specific reason to amplify text.

Sentences and paragraphs

A clear sentence is short and to the point. A typical length is between 10 and 14 words. Try to present one idea only in each sentence.

A sentence consists of a subject and a predicate. The subject (noun or pronoun) is the thing, person or idea that the sentence is about. The predicate says something about the subject. It includes the verb i.e. the action of the sentence, what the subject is doing or what is being done to the subject.

Sentences may also include an object, which is the thing or person affected by the action of the verb.

Paragraphs are a collection of sentences that together focus on a single point, argument or thought. It should develop one main idea through these related sentences. It should not be too long: no more than four or five sentences and 200 words. If your text includes bullets and displayed content, your paragraphs might be shorter. For emphasis, a paragraph might be a single sentence. A text that is composed of several short paragraphs with indentions or a blank line between each is easier to read than one with lots of long lines of dense prose.

Punctuation

Punctuation marks are helpful aids for the reader. They exist to help the reader make sense of a text. They help structure a sentence and prevent ambiguity or confusion. A classic example is the title of Lynne Truss's book *Eats, Shoots and Leaves*. The meaning is different depending on where the commas appear.

The panda *eats shoots and leaves*. [He eats both the shoots and leaves of a plant].

The gangster *eats* [his meal], *shoots* [his gun] and *leaves* [the crime scene].

The monkey *eats shoots*, and [then] *leaves*.

Be particularly careful in legal documents or when referring to areas of responsibility or financial information. Avoid peppering your text with punctuation marks. A sentence full of commas between short phrases suggests that the sentence is too long. Often, two shorter sentences are better at conveying meaning than one longer one.

The punctuation marks you are likely to need appear in the table below.

Punctuation mark	Name	Used ...	Notes
.	full stop	at the end of a sentence; in abbreviations	also called a full point
,	comma	in a sentence to indicate a pause and to aid the reader to make sense of the text; in a list of words	try not to create sentences that have lots of commas: rework the sentence to make it shorter
-	hyphen	in words that are composed of two other words	e.g. *high-rise*
–	dash	to set apart two ideas	e.g. The sales rep – the one from Berlin – arrives tonight.
( )	brackets	around text that might be supplementary to a main point	also [ ] square brackets
...	three-dot ellipsis	to indicate that something from a text is omitted, used mainly in direct quotations from another source	can be spaced ... or unspaced ...
' '	quotation or speech marks	around direct speech that you might quote, for example in a press release; used to highlight a specific term, particularly one that might be new to the reader	can also be doubles " " e.g. the so-called "diamond effect". US English uses double quote marks for speech

'	apostrophe	in contractions: don't (= shorthand for 'do not'); to show the possessive: the executive's office (= the office of the executive)	it is NOT needed in dates (1950's) or in plurals (photo's)
?	question mark	in direct questions and rhetorical questions (ones that don't require an answer)	when used well, say in a series of short, punchy direct questions, it can be effective and immediate
/	forward slash	to show two or more options; it is similar to using 'and'	spaces can be added between the dash and the following or preceding letters, or the letters may be closed up: and / or; he/she/they
:	colon	to introduce a list: pen, pencil, ruler, paper; or to balance two complementary or similar ideas	e.g. there are two options: sell, or sit tight. if you don't know how to use one, keep your sentences simple and avoid colons
;	semi-colon	similar to a comma, but providing more of a pause, connecting two related, but independent clauses	e.g. Rashid spent three hours at the market; he couldn't find what he needed. if you don't know how to use one, keep your sentences simple and avoid semi-colons

Never use the exclamation mark (!) in formal writing. It is for exclamations: *Pow! Wham! Ouch!* Unless you are authoring a graphic novel, it is very unlikely you will need to use them.

Spelling

Many English words are like each other in how they sound or are spelled. The differences can be subtle but meaning can be affected if you use the wrong word. An example of this is adverse and averse, which both mean 'opposed'. Adverse (usually used before a noun) means unfavourable:

His social media post brought the company adverse publicity.

Averse (verb) describes a person who is reluctant to do something:

He has been averse to carrying out the instructions given to him.

If in doubt, avoid such words. The sentences could be rewritten like this:

His social media post provided the company with negative publicity.

He refuses to carry out the instructions given to him.

Watch out for words that are particularly close in spelling. Climatic and climactic are divided by only the letter 'c', but have very different meanings. Your spell checker might not pick up that you have used them interchangeably as they are both legitimate words.

The conference drew to a climactic close, with a hard-hitting speech on the severe climatic changes that have been created by global warming.

Sloppy spelling in a document can reflect badly on a writer or company whose logo is emblazoned across it. Check that you mean to use *waive* not *wave*, *troop* not *troupe*, *cannon* not *canon*, *straight* not *strait*.

Confusing words

Watch out for these commonly confused words. The spellings and meanings can get muddled. If in doubt, leave them out of your writing altogether.

Word 1	Meaning	Word 2	Meaning
affect	verb, to influence, change	effect	verb, to succeed in carrying out, impact
fewer	used with nouns that can be counted, e.g. fewer meetings	less	used with nouns that can't be counted, e.g. less time
their	possessive, belonging to, e.g. their views	there	position, place e.g. over there
it's	it is (contraction)	its	belonging to
stationary	not moving	stationery	paper and pens
practice	noun	practise	verb
accept	to agree to	except	excluding
amount / quantity	used with singular words that have no plural	number	used with plural nouns that can be counted
biannual	twice a year	biennial	every two years
altogether	completely, in total	all together	everyone
beside	next to	besides	in addition to
lose	mislay, fail to win	loose	not fixed, free
principle	ethical standard	principal	main or primary
formerly	previously	formally	officially

TOP TIP

Clear, exact text devoid of errors means your reader can digest your content.

Sloppy grammatical and spelling mistakes might (rightly or wrongly) suggest your thoughts and ideas are also ill-formed and unreliable.

George Orwell, novelist, journalist and polemicist, gave this good advice:

- never use a long word where a short one will do;

- if it is possible to cut a word out, always cut it out;

- Never use the passive voice where you can use the active voice;

- Never use a foreign phrase, a scientific word or a jargon word if you can think of an everyday English equivalent.

COMMON MISTAKES

✗ You don't proofread your writing. Mistakes will distract readers from your key message, make you look unprofessional and could make it more difficult for the reader to understand your writing.

✗ Your sentences are too long and full of commas. Consider reworking them to make use of full stops, semi-colons or colons, which will give your writing more punch. Make sure you know how to use them, though!

✗ You use the passive voice too often. Statements will have far more impact if you use the active voice.

✗ You use the wrong words. Take some time to make sure you're clear about the difference between commonly confused words such as *effect* and *affect*, or *forward* and *foreword*.

BUSINESS ESSENTIALS

✔ Make sure you have a good grasp of spelling and grammar. If you're unsure, turn to the resources at the back of this book for a list of helpful guides.

✔ If you have time, ask a colleague to proofread your writing. It's very difficult to self-edit and people often don't spot mistakes in their own work.

✔ Don't rely on your computer spell check – it won't pick up on legitimate words that you've used incorrectly.

✔ Take the time to review your work after your first draft, and think about whether you could shorten sentences or use punctuation for more impact.

8
Recap: Writing rules – essential dos

This book is mostly not about rules. Being overly prescriptive about how you put words together can be too restrictive. It's a good idea to understand the basics of how language works and to adhere to the standard principles, but as any seasoned writer will happily tell you, rules are there to be broken.

The earlier chapters in this book emphasized the need to assess what your writing is for: who will read it and how and why you are putting it in front of them? What result are you aiming for?

If you have a good grasp of what your intentions are, then you are off to a flying start. This chapter, beyond all the others, is one you should not skip. It is the nearest it comes to stating fundamental rules of written communication. Stick to the advice given here and your writing will be clearer, punchier and more immediate and thus more effective.

As in other chapters, we are starting with the reader and not with the writer. The writer is the messenger. There is no room for self-conscious prose and convoluted sentences in information writing. In all forms of transactional writing – with the notable exception of selling copy – the intention is to persuade your reader to read on. You want them to engage with your text from the first few lines and to continue reading uninterrupted.

Keep things simple

If you find writing a challenge, then sticking to grammatical and linguistic rules might help you. Developing a vocabulary that is precise and clear and sentences that are short and to the point will enhance your confidence. 'Good' writing is writing that readers can understand.

Use simple words and avoid over-lengthy sentences, full of subordinate clauses and asides, divided by commas, and that are not relevant to the point or argument you are trying to make, as they may lose your reader's attention.

For example, sentences like the previous one. This could instead be written like this:

Use simple and direct words to get your message across. Long sentences full of unnecessary detail can confuse your reader.

Divide the long sentence into two shorter sentences, keeping a single idea in each. The points are positive rather than highlighting what not to do. Remove some detail that doesn't add to the sense of the point being made. The text is easier to read as a result.

Finding the right word to use is important. If a software system your company is using has become outdated and is no longer fit for purpose, say so. It is a straightforward term. These other words have roughly the same meaning – antiquated, archaic, obsolete, passé, antediluvian – but they draw unnecessary attention to themselves and won't be familiar to all readers. They may get in the way of what you are trying to say. Put your thesaurus away, stop showing off and keep things simple.

The essential dos of writing

- Write in the active voice. (See p. 58.)
- Use the present tense. (See p. 72.)
- Have a beginning, middle and end: a clear structure for what you want to convey.
- Cultivate the art of concision and precision.
- Write in full sentences. All sentences must contain a verb, start with a capital letter, end with a full stop and make sense.
- Be positive, not negative. (See pp. 56–57.)
- Cut redundancy. Filler phrases will slow down a text and may make it muddled and flabby. There will be linguistic tics that you use in everyday speech: try not to use them in your written communication where they will be unnecessary and too informal. This includes phrases such as: aka, let's agree to disagree, at the end of the day, it goes without saying.

Avoid:

- slang, dialect, region-specific terms;
- using two words when one will do;
- clichés and jargon (See pp. 62–63);
- should, would, could, may and might – the conditional tense is too hesitant for business prose;

- words that don't mean much without contextual explanation: holistic, paradigm shift, woke, agile;
- anything that makes your writing long-winded or complicated;
- subordinate clauses;
- long sentences and paragraphs (see pp. 73–74);
- irrelevant asides – if necessary, you can include information that supports your main points or argument in an appendix;
- terms that might be confusing to those for whom English is not a first language;
- culturally insensitive references;
- derogatory terms that are sexist, racism, ageist or offensive in other ways.

Don't:

- try to be funny;
- use the exclamation mark;
- start a sentence with and, or, or but;
- end a sentence with a preposition.

Words on the screen or page are powerful tools at your disposal in a business context. Use them wisely and with care.

9
Checking and editing your work

Reviewing and checking your writing can improve your text. Software checkers, style guides and templates can help.

Avoiding mistakes

There is no excuse for allow spelling or grammatical mistakes to get through into the final version of your text.

There are spelling and grammar checkers built into most writing software. However, watch out for these and know what you are asking them to check.

You need to allow time to read through your writing to pick up last-minute mistakes. The odd typo in an internal memo or plan might be acceptable; in a document for external consumption, such as an annual report, it is not acceptable. If you don't have a team whose task is to check documents pre-publication, then consider buddying up with a colleague informally to review each other's text. You'll be surprised what you pick up.

The human eye is adept at reading what it wants to read. Letters in a certain order might fool your brain into thinking the word in question is another one completely.

Checking software

If you write in Word and similar software, it's a good idea to use the checking tools within its Editor suite, though ensure you the checker is set to your preferred form of English – British or US. You can use these to check for grammar, spelling and readability.

Templates

If you have standard documents or emails that you and colleagues use or send regularly, setting up some templates is a good idea. These are helpful because they:

- help enforce consistency;

- prompt you for content that needs to be included;

- are efficient and save time – you don't need to 'reinvent' the format each time you need to create a document;

- have an established set of rules regarding layout, style of headings, order of sections to conform to;

- instil confidence in those who receive the document;

- help focus your thoughts on what is essential for inclusion and what is surplus.

Example: A company commissions work regularly from a third party.

Originally, each person who commissioned the work created their own emails. To ensure that all the necessary details are provided to a standard style, the following template was created:

Dear delivery team,

Please create introductory text and keywords for this title as an XML file.

TITLE: The Last Frontier
AUTHOR: Lucy Ann Carey
PRODUCT: NPT
ORIGIN: US
Subject: Cultural Studies
Number of Chapters: 12
Special Requirements: n/a
MS: in Word, attached as zip file
Return date: 15-03-22

The invoice should be sent to james.bloom@workplace.com – James Bloom.

The PO reference is: NPT00345

With thanks,

Pam, Commissioning Team (UK)

Style guides

If your organization regularly produces lengthy documents and reports that are circulated widely and outside the company, you should consider drawing up a set of set of guidelines that you can adhere to each time you write a new document.

It should include rules on what to follow so that you and your colleagues create professional, consistently styled content. A rule book like this means you don't need to think about aspects of spelling and abbreviations and other styles each time you start a document: they are already enshrined in your company's culture. Style guides can be an important way to enforce your brand.

If you work in a publishing, media, brand or marketing role, it is likely that you already refer to a style guide or have a written house style.

Your style guide can include various principles.

Spelling: whether you use British or US English, e.g. colour v color; -ise or -ize verbs: standardise or standardize; modern or more arcane forms: focused or focussed.

Abbreviations: whether you allow them (Bucks for Buckinghamshire; 19th century for nineteenth century; km for kilometres) or have a rule always to write terms out in full when first used in a chapter or a report.

Formality: whether you allow contractions or not: would not v wouldn't; when you use capitals for certain terms, e.g. postmodernism or Postmodernism.

Punctuation and spacing: if this is used in abbreviations, e.g. i.e. v ie; in sentences, e.g. ... v . . . ; using colons before lists; using the 'Oxford' comma in lists: paper, pens, erasers, and booklets.

Words or symbols: e.g. whether to use per cent or percentage or % – all are acceptable in most contexts; sticking to one makes a text clear and professional.

The guidelines could include specific examples to be followed for: numbers, dates, measurements, times. E.g. 2nd September 2023 v 2 Sept 2023; eighty-three v 83; 23m v 23 metres or meters.

Professional editors and proof readers

Unless you work in a large organization or one that produces publications or documents for public consumption, it is unlikely that you will have staff on hand to review and check text. Even in the book and newspaper sectors, the close checking work is usually done by freelance editors. These might be:

Copyeditors who check that text ('copy') makes sense, has no spelling, punctuation or grammatical errors, and ensure text is readable. A copyeditor will usually edit documents with track changes on so suggested changes to the original text can be seen.

Sub-editors rewrite, shorten and enhance text to make it punchier and more readable and are employed by ad and brand agencies, newspapers and magazines to turn a journalist's raw prose into text that fits the style and tone of a publication. They will also add in straplines and will work to strict word counts.

Proof readers are usually the last to check a text once it has been completed or 'typeset' in the format, font and design in which it will appear as a published document. A proof reader will read for sense and do final checks to see if any spelling errors (typos) have slipped through.

For publicity and sales copy, if you have time and budget, asking a professional to read and review your text is recommended.

Always share your house style, if you have one, with external editors so they can follow this.

Reading back over your work

Don't just rely on others to check your work. You know what you want to say and why you need to communicate it. You are in the best position to read back over your own writing to check that it fulfils the brief you set yourself. Does it adhere to the advice set out in this book?

Take pride in your writing and in perfecting it.

> **TOP TIP**
>
> It can help to read your words out loud. You may pick up errors you miss on the page.
>
> If you have time, it's helpful to put your draft text away for an hour or a day. When you read it afresh you will spot mistakes and inappropriate language that you failed to notice before.

Test it out

Ask a willing colleague to read your text, preferably someone who has a similar level of knowledge or understanding of the topic as your intended audience.

- Can they follow it clearly?
- Is the level and tone right?
- Did they keep reading to the end?
- Were they engaged with your writing?

As you want constructive feedback, it's always a good idea to ask someone whose opinion you trust. Try not to see comments in a negative way: use them to improve your text.

Checklists

These checklists are useful reminders when you have a document to create.

Checklist 1: Preparing your document

Have you asked yourself:

- who is my audience?
- why am I communicating with my audience?
- what is the purpose of my report or correspondence?
- how can I best communicate? (It may not be by written text.)
- what are the key points I want and need to get across?
- how do I want my audience to respond?

Checklist 2: Asking for constructive feedback on your text

For longer pieces of writing, such as a report or business plan, it's a good idea to ask someone else to take a look and give helpful advice on how the text might be improved.

Ask the test reader the following questions. This is particularly useful if you are working on a document with multiple authors.

- Is it clear what the document is for? Is the main message apparent?

- Does it match the intention and purpose I have set out?
- Is the text clear and easy to follow?
- Are there any areas of communication I could improve upon: expand or rephrase?
- Is the text engaging enough and have I set the right tone?
- Is anything crucial missing?
- Is there any jargon or terminology I should explain?
- Is the structure logical and the document easy to navigate?
- Are there any other comments you would like to add?
- Would you be happy to look at a revised draft after I've collated your comments and those of other colleagues?

Checklist 3: Layout and structure

Consider including:

- bullets and numbered lists;
- a glossary of key terms used;
- visual elements to explain or show data;
- an abstract or digest at the top of the document;
- both shortened and longer versions of a document for different readers;
- fonts and styles to make some text stand out.

Remember to include in longer documents:

- page numbering;
- headings for navigation; these might be numbered;
- a contents list for ease of navigation;

- headers and footers;
- version and authoring details;
- a logical structure.

Checklist 4: Clarity and sense

Have you:

- used clear, short sentences and paragraphs?
- used the active voice?
- removed any words that are too flowery or not well known?
- checked your argument is easy to follow?

Checklist 5: Spelling, grammar and punctuation

Before you send or share a document, particularly one that is representing you, your team or your organization externally, check that you have:

- amended spelling errors;
- looked out for muddled verb tenses;
- deleted unnecessary adjectives;
- been consistent in the use of English – all US or all British?
- checked grammar and punctuation is correct;
- removed jargon, clichés or esoteric words that some readers may not understand;
- ensured facts and statistics are correct and up to date;
- checked names of people and places, titles and affiliations are accurate;
- made sure URLs are true and active;
- confirmed sources for any quotations used.

Where to find more help

Dictionaries and thesauri

A good, up-to-date dictionary is a writer's best friend.
There are plenty to choose from including:
US English – Merriam-Webster www.merriam-webster.com/
British English – Collins www.collinsdictionary.com/
International – Cambridge University Press https://
dictionary.cambridge.org/dictionary/

Guides to style

New Oxford Dictionary for Writers and Editors
(OUP, 2014)
New Hart's Rules: The Oxford Style Guide (OUP, 2nd edn
2014)
Chicago Manual of Style www.chicagomanualofstyle.org/

Editing software

After the Deadline https://afterthedeadline.com/
Grammarly www.grammarly.com/
ProWritingAid https://prowritingaid.com/

Grammar and usage

*The Right Word: A Writer's Toolkit of Grammar,
Vocabulary and Literary Terms* (Bloomsbury, 2021)

Practical advice

The Plain English Campaign www.plainenglish.co.uk/
Chartered Institute of Editing and Proofreading
www.ciep.uk/

Index